Baby Animals

by Cindy Chapman

Reading Consultant: Wiley Blevins, M.A.
Phonics/Early Reading Specialist

 COMPASS POINT BOOKS

Minneapolis, Minnesota

Compass Point Books
3109 West 50th Street, #115
Minneapolis, MN 55410

Visit Compass Point Books on the Internet at *www.compasspointbooks.com*
or e-mail your request to *custserv@compasspointbooks.com*

Photographs ©: Cover: Image Source/elektraVision, p. 1: Image Source/elektraVision,
p. 6: Image Source/elektraVision, p. 7: Ron Kimball Photography, p. 8: Corbis/Frank Lane
Picture Agency/Michael Rose, p. 9: Corbis/Kit Houghton, p. 10: Bruce Coleman, Inc./John
Hyde, p. 11: Stockbyte, p. 12: Brand X Pictures/Elyse Lewin

Editorial Development: Alice Dickstein, Alice Boynton
Photo Researcher: Wanda Winch
Design/Page Production: Silver Editions, Inc.

Library of Congress Cataloging-in-Publication Data
Chapman, Cindy.
    Baby animals / by Cindy Chapman.
        p. cm. — (Compass Point phonics readers)
    Summary: Briefly introduces a variety of baby animals, in a text
    that incorporates phonics instruction and rebuses.
    Includes bibliographical references and index.
    ISBN 0-7565-0504-6 (hardcover : alk. paper)
        1. Animals—Infancy—Juvenile literature. 2. Reading—Phonetic
    method—Juvenile literature.   [1. Animals—Infancy. 2. Rebuses.
    3. Reading—Phonetic method.]   I. Title. II. Series.
    QL763.C465 2003
    591.3'9—dc21   2003006348

Table of Contents

Dear Parent or Caregiver,

Welcome to Compass Point Phonics Readers, books of information for young children. Each book concentrates on specific phonic sounds and words commonly found in beginning reading materials. Featuring eye-catching photographs, every book explores a single science or social studies concept that is sure to grab a child's interest.

So snuggle up with your child, and let's begin. Start by reading aloud the Mother Goose nursery rhyme on the next page. As you read, stress the words in dark type. These are the words that contain the phonic sounds featured in this book. After several readings, pause before the rhyming words, and let your child chime in.

Now let's read *Baby Animals*. If your child is a beginning reader, have him or her first read it silently. Then ask your child to read it aloud. For children who are not yet reading, read the book aloud as you run your finger under the words. Ask your child to imitate, or "echo," what he or she has just heard.

Discussing the book's content with your child:
Explain to your child that some animals go through amazing changes as they grow from being a baby to an adult. Tadpoles, for example, are born in water, so they have tails to help them swim. As tadpoles grow into frogs, they develop lungs so that they can move around.

At the back of the book is a fun Nice Going! game. Your child will take pride in demonstrating his or her mastery of the phonic sounds and the high-frequency words.

Enjoy Compass Point Phonics Readers and watch your child read and learn!

Barber, Barber

Barber, barber, shave a **pig,**
How many hairs to make a **wig?**
Four and twenty, that's enough
To dance a **jig** and **trim** a cuff.

It can wag its  tail .
But it is not a big cat.

It can yip and yap.
But it is not a big dog.

It will hop a lot.
But it is not a big .

It is fast.
But it is not a big .

It can swim.
But it is not a big seal.

It has a bill.
But it is not a big duck .

It will get big and read.
What is it?

Word List

Short *i*

is

it(s)

swim

will

yip

c

can

cat

d

and

dog

w

wag

will

y

yap

yip

High-Frequency

big

but

get

read

Science

animals

baby

bill

Nice Going!

You will need:
- 1 penny
- 2 moving pieces, such as nickels or checkers

Player 1

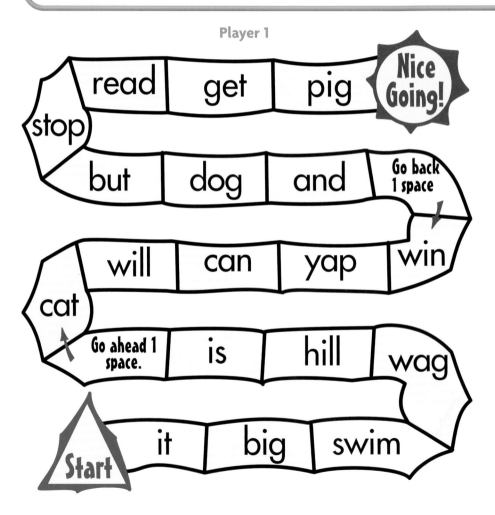

read | get | pig | **Nice Going!**

stop

but | dog | and | Go back 1 space

win | yap | can | will

cat

Go ahead 1 space. | is | hill | wag

it | big | swim

Start

14

How to Play

- Each player puts a moving piece on his or her Start. Players take turns shaking the penny and dropping it on the table. Heads means move 1 space. Tails means move 2 spaces.
- The player moves and reads the word in the space. If the child cannot read the word, tell him or her what it is. On the next turn, the child must read the word before moving.
- If a player lands on a space having special directions, he or she should move accordingly.
- The first player to reach the *Nice Going!* sign wins the game.

Player 2

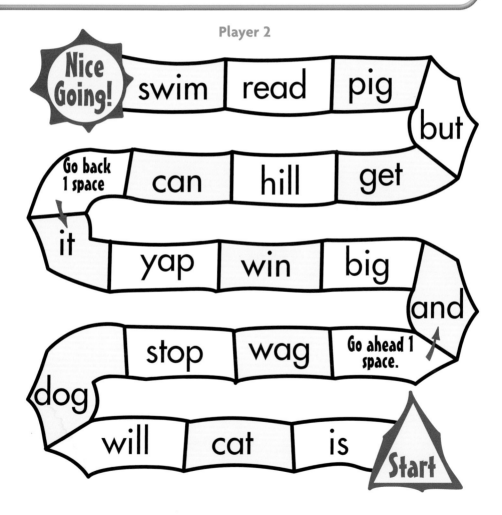

Read More

Frost, Helen. *Baby Birds.* Mankato, Minn.: Pebble Books, 1999.

Saunders-Smith, Gail. *Frogs.* Animals: Life Cycles Series. Mankato, Minn.: Pebble Books, 1998.

Stone, Lynn M. *Horses Have Foals.* Minneapolis, Minn.: Compass Point Books, 2000.

Tafuri, Nancy. *Mama's Little Bears.* New York: Scholastic, 2002.

Index